Cybersecurity Basics for Beginners

Understand Online Threats, Password Protection, and How to Stay Safe in a Connected World

By Joe Correa

Published by Live Stronger Faster

This book is for educational and informational purposes only. The author and publisher are not engaged in rendering legal, financial, or other professional advice. Readers should consult a qualified professional before making any financial decisions.

First Edition

Table of Contents

Introduction 5

Chapter 1: What Is Cybersecurity and Why It Matters 8

Chapter 2: Passwords, Passphrases & Protecting Your Logins 18

Chapter 3: Recognizing Scams, Phishing, and Social Engineering Attacks 28

Chapter 4: Securing Your Devices — Phones, Computers, and Tablets 37

Chapter 5: Safe Internet Browsing and Securing Your Online Activity 46

Chapter 6: Protecting Your Personal Data and Privacy Online 55

Chapter 7: Securing Your Email, Messaging, and Social Media Accounts 64

Chapter 8: Protecting Your Children and Family Online 73

Chapter 9: Recognizing and Responding to Identity Theft 81

Chapter 10: Building a Lifelong Cybersecurity Mindset 90

Epilogue: A Safer You Starts Now 99

Introduction

We live in a world that is more connected than ever before. From smart thermostats and fitness trackers to online banking and business data stored in the cloud, our personal and professional lives are deeply woven into the digital landscape. While this convenience offers incredible opportunities, it also opens the door to unprecedented risks. Every day, millions of people unknowingly expose themselves to hackers, phishing scams, identity theft, and data breaches, not because they're careless, but because they simply don't know what to look out for. That's where this book, and this series, begins.

Cybersecurity Basics for Beginners is your friendly, no-jargon-required guide to understanding the digital threats around you and learning how to protect yourself and your information. This book was written for regular people — not tech experts. Whether you're a parent trying to keep your kids safe online, a business owner who needs to secure client data, or someone who just wants to stop getting hacked and scammed, you're in the right place.

Cybersecurity isn't just for IT departments and government agencies. It's for everyone. In fact, cybercriminals often rely on ignorance and complacency. They don't need to "hack" sophisticated systems when they can simply trick someone into clicking a bad link or reusing the same weak password across dozens of accounts. The truth is, most security breaches are preventable with the right habits, tools, and awareness — and that's exactly what this book will teach you.

We'll start with the basics: what cybersecurity really means, the types of threats you might face, and why it's more urgent now than ever before. From there, we'll break down what makes a strong password (and how to remember it), how to spot phishing emails and fake websites, and how to use two-factor authentication and VPNs to lock down your data like a pro. You'll also learn how to protect your devices, networks, and even your family members, using simple, low-cost strategies.

The goal of this book is not to overwhelm you with tech-speak or scare you into paranoia. It's to empower you with practical steps you can take immediately — even if you've never thought of yourself as "tech-savvy." You don't need a degree in computer science to stay safe online. You just need the right mindset and the right information, delivered in a clear and actionable way.

This is Book 1 in the *Cyber Shield Academy* series, a 10-part journey from beginner to cyber-proficient. Each book in the series is designed to help you master a key area of cybersecurity and digital privacy — from understanding threats and securing your devices, to protecting your small business, mastering secure communication, and navigating data privacy laws. You'll get practical tools, real-world examples, and step-by-step guidance to build your cyber confidence, one topic at a time.

Before we get started, here's one thing to remember: cyber threats may be growing, but so is your ability to outsmart them. This book is the first step in reclaiming your power in the digital world. The internet is here to stay — and so are the risks — but with the right shield, you can stay safe, confident, and in control.

Let's begin your cybersecurity journey.

Chapter 1: What Is Cybersecurity and Why It Matters

Understanding Cybersecurity: The Modern Battlefield

Cybersecurity is the practice of protecting computers, servers, mobile devices, networks, and data from malicious attacks. In today's connected world, nearly everything we do — from banking and shopping to chatting and working — relies on digital systems. These systems make life easier, but they also create vulnerabilities. Cybersecurity acts as the invisible armor we wear to shield our digital presence from theft, exploitation, and destruction.

Think of cybersecurity as both a personal hygiene routine and a national defense system. On a small scale, it's about using strong passwords, locking your phone, and avoiding suspicious links. On a larger scale, it includes protecting hospitals from ransomware attacks, shielding power grids from foreign intrusions, and defending small businesses from customer data breaches. Whether you're an individual or an organization, cybersecurity is your front line of defense.

The Real-World Risks: It's Not "If," It's "When"

Many people wrongly assume that cyberattacks only happen to large companies or the ultra-wealthy. But in reality, most attacks target ordinary individuals and small businesses. Why? Because they're easy targets. They often don't have advanced security, and hackers can automate mass attacks to exploit weak spots.

If you've ever had a social media account hacked, received a suspicious email from "your bank," or seen strange charges on your credit card, you've already experienced the risks firsthand. Cybercriminals use everything from email phishing and fake websites to malware hidden in apps and free downloads. These tactics don't require much effort but can steal your identity, drain your bank account, or compromise your reputation.

Cybersecurity is no longer optional. The threat landscape is evolving every day — and it's your job to stay one step ahead. Learning the basics is the first and most critical step.

The Core Pillars of Cybersecurity

Cybersecurity is built on several key pillars that work together to form a complete protection system. The first is confidentiality — keeping sensitive information private and out of the wrong hands. This includes everything from your passwords and Social Security number to business documents and medical records. Without confidentiality, trust in digital systems disappears.

Next is integrity — ensuring that data remains accurate and unaltered unless authorized. Imagine if a hacker could change your banking records, medical history, or employment file without you knowing. Maintaining data integrity ensures that what's stored is what's real.

Then comes **availability** — ensuring that information and systems are accessible to the right people when they need them. Denial-of-service (DoS) attacks, for instance, can bring down entire websites or services. High availability is crucial for both businesses and users who rely on real-time access.

When you hear about cybersecurity, you're really hearing about the protection of these three principles: confidentiality, integrity, and availability — also known as the "CIA Triad."

Cybercriminals: Who Are They and What Do They Want?

Not all hackers wear hoodies and live in basements. In fact, cybercriminals come in many forms — and not all of them are human. Some are lone-wolf hackers working for personal gain, while others are state-sponsored groups conducting digital warfare. Some use ransomware to lock systems and demand payment. Others are scammers pretending to be your bank or employer. Still others deploy bots and AI-powered scripts to target thousands of users at once.

Their motivations vary. Some want money, plain and simple. Others want political influence, revenge, access to intellectual property, or even social clout in the dark web underworld. Some attacks are random, while others are highly targeted and sophisticated. The more you understand the mindset of a cybercriminal, the better you can protect yourself.

This chapter isn't about fear — it's about awareness. Once you recognize the different types of threats and the people behind them, you begin to take back control.

The Cost of Ignorance: Personal and Professional Consequences

The consequences of ignoring cybersecurity go far beyond a hacked Facebook account. On a personal level, your identity can be stolen, your bank drained, your credit ruined, or your photos leaked. On a professional level, a single data breach can destroy a company's reputation, trigger lawsuits, or result in devastating financial penalties.

For example, a small business owner might lose all customer data due to a phishing attack, leading to lost clients and potential lawsuits. A freelancer might have their entire portfolio wiped out by ransomware. Even a single click on the wrong link can unleash malware that spreads across devices and networks.

Cybersecurity isn't just a tech issue — it's a life issue. It affects your finances, your job, your family, and your peace of mind. The more proactive you are, the less reactive you'll need to be when something goes wrong.

A Beginner's Mindset: You Don't Need to Be a Tech Genius

The good news is that learning cybersecurity basics doesn't require a tech degree or coding skills. What it does require is awareness, habit-building, and a willingness to take responsibility for your digital life. Just like locking your doors at night, practicing cybersecurity should become second nature.

Start by understanding the value of your information. Every email, password, login, or photo is a potential entry point for a cybercriminal. Next, get into the habit of questioning everything: Is this email really from who it says it's from? Is this website secure? Is my password too easy to guess? These small shifts in mindset can have massive protective effects.

This chapter sets the stage for the rest of the book — and the entire series. You'll move from basic protection strategies to advanced practices over time. But no matter how far you go, remember: cybersecurity begins with a choice — to take your digital safety seriously.

The Wake-Up Call

Sophia never thought much about cybersecurity. She was a freelance writer in her early thirties, working from home in a cozy apartment just outside Seattle. Her mornings usually began with a cup of coffee, a scroll through social media, and diving into whatever client project was on her plate that day. Life was simple and digital. Like most people, she reused passwords, clicked "Remind me later" on software updates, and assumed antivirus software from five years ago was still running somewhere in the background.

One Monday morning, she opened her laptop to find something strange. A flashing red screen had replaced her desktop. A message read: **"Your files have been encrypted. Pay $1,200 in Bitcoin to unlock your data."** Her stomach dropped. She tried clicking out, but it was no use. All her documents — articles, contracts, even personal photos — were locked. She didn't understand how it had happened. And that was the worst part: she had no idea where to even start.

As the hours passed, panic set in. She called her tech-savvy friend Mike, who quickly explained that she'd likely fallen victim to ransomware — a type of cyberattack where hackers lock your files and demand payment. "Did you click on anything weird lately?" he asked.

Sophia remembered an email from what looked like her client's company. It had a subject line that said "Invoice Attached" and even used her client's name. Without thinking, she clicked the link and opened a file that looked like a spreadsheet. That was three days ago.

Mike sighed. "That's probably it. They're using phishing emails now that look really convincing. It's not your fault, but next time you've gotta double-check the sender and never open random attachments."

Sophia felt foolish. She wasn't some reckless teenager on sketchy websites. She was just trying to do her job. But somehow, she'd let someone walk right through her digital front door — and now everything was at risk.

Over the next few days, Sophia learned more about cybersecurity than she had in her entire life. She started watching YouTube videos, reading articles, and listening to podcasts about cyber hygiene. The more she learned, the angrier she became — not just at the hackers, but at herself for assuming she didn't need to worry about it.

She discovered that over **300,000 new malware programs are created daily**, that **phishing scams cost billions annually**, and that **60% of small businesses fail within 6 months of a cyberattack**. And here she was, a one-woman business, completely vulnerable and totally unprepared.

Sophia had always considered herself smart. She never thought a "hacker" would bother with someone like her. But that's the point — cybercriminals aren't always targeting high-profile targets. They want easy wins. People who won't notice until it's too late. And this time, she had been the jackpot.

After a few sleepless nights and more coffee than she cared to admit, Sophia made a decision: she wouldn't pay the ransom. Mike helped her wipe the hard drive and restore what she could from old cloud backups. She lost about 30% of her work — including some personal writing she hadn't saved anywhere else. But she considered it tuition. The price she had to pay for her digital naivety.

More importantly, she made a vow to never be caught off guard again.

She began taking practical steps. She installed a password manager and created long, unique passphrases for every account. She enabled two-factor authentication on her email, bank, and social media. She updated her software regularly. She even started using a VPN when working in cafés or co-working spaces.

Her friends joked that she had turned into a cybersecurity nut. But Sophia just smiled. She wasn't paranoid — she was prepared.

That one attack became a turning point in her career. She began pitching articles on cybersecurity for freelancers, writing guides for remote workers, and even creating content for tech startups focused on online safety. Her painful lesson had given her a new niche — and a purpose.

One of her most popular posts was titled *"It'll Never Happen to Me — Until It Does."* She shared her story openly and received hundreds of messages from others who had gone through similar experiences. Some had their savings drained. Others had their online businesses hijacked. All of them had one thing in common: they had no idea how easy it was for someone to break in until it was too late.

Sophia realized that cybersecurity wasn't just a tech topic — it was a human topic. It was about people, trust, and the very real consequences of being unprotected in a digital world.

Months later, Sophia's apartment looked the same — but something fundamental had changed. She no longer ignored software updates or used the same password twice. She no longer saw online threats as something for "other people" to worry about. She had learned, the hard way, that cybersecurity is everyone's responsibility.

And now, when she helped others build their online presence, she started with one question: *"How are you protecting your digital life?"*

Because behind every click, every email, and every login, there's a decision being made — to stay vulnerable or to stay aware.

Sophia chose awareness. And that choice made all the difference.

Chapter 2: Passwords, Passphrases & Protecting Your Logins

Why Passwords Are Still the Front Door to Your Digital Life

Passwords are the oldest form of digital security, yet they remain one of the weakest links in personal cybersecurity. Every app, email, bank, and cloud account begins with a simple login — a username and password. But if that one line of defense is weak, everything behind it is exposed.

Many people assume that cybercriminals are cracking passwords using advanced algorithms, but the truth is often simpler — attackers exploit human behavior. People tend to reuse passwords, use easily guessable words (like "password123"), or store them in unsafe ways. That's why a huge percentage of hacks begin with compromised credentials. In fact, over 80% of data breaches are tied to weak or reused passwords. Strengthening your login practices is one of the easiest and most impactful ways to protect yourself online.

The Anatomy of a Strong Password vs. a Strong Passphrase

There's a difference between a password and a passphrase. A **password** is often a single word or string of characters — think "Summer2024!" or "Johnny!123". A **passphrase** is a longer sentence-like string, such as

"GiraffesDanceAtMidnight2025!" or "ILoveMyDogRufus&CoffeeDaily." Passphrases are harder to guess, easier to remember, and significantly more secure.

Strong passwords or passphrases should follow three principles: length, complexity, and uniqueness. **Length** is critical — longer is better. **Complexity** means mixing uppercase and lowercase letters, numbers, and special symbols. **Uniqueness** means never reusing a password across multiple accounts. A strong passphrase could be a combination of unrelated words, a quirky sentence, or a phrase only you would understand. Avoid names, birth dates, or anything personally identifiable.

Using one master password or phrase for everything is like using the same key for your house, car, mailbox, and office — lose it once, and everything's compromised.

The Danger of Reusing Passwords Across Accounts

It's tempting to reuse a password, especially for accounts that don't seem "important." But hackers don't discriminate. They often start with the least secure platforms — like a food delivery app or an old forum login — and work their way into your core accounts.

This strategy is called **credential stuffing** – attackers take stolen usernames and passwords from data breaches and automatically test them on other sites, hoping you've reused them. If your password from a fitness app was leaked last year and you used the same one for your Gmail, you could wake up one day to find your email hijacked, your bank accessed, or your social media accounts deleted.

Using unique passwords for every account is essential, especially for email, banking, cloud storage, and work-related platforms. These are high-value targets that can lead to serious personal and financial damage if compromised.

How to Manage Passwords Without Going Crazy

With dozens or even hundreds of accounts, how can anyone possibly remember unique passwords for each? The answer: **password managers.** A password manager is a secure digital vault that stores and generates strong, unique passwords for every account. You only need to remember one master password to access the vault.

Popular password managers like **1Password**, **Bitwarden**, and **LastPass** encrypt your data and sync across devices. They can automatically fill in logins, suggest strong new passwords, and alert you to weak or reused ones. Using a password manager not only increases your security, it simplifies your digital life.

If you're not ready to commit to a full password manager, start with a hybrid approach: use a notebook stored securely in your home (never online), or begin using passphrases that follow a personal formula only you understand. Just avoid writing passwords on sticky notes or saving them in browser notes, emails, or unencrypted cloud files.

Adding a Second Lock: Two-Factor Authentication (2FA)

Even the strongest password can be compromised. That's why **two-factor authentication (2FA)** is a must for any important account. 2FA adds an extra step after you enter your password — usually a one-time code sent via text, email, or an authenticator app like **Google Authenticator** or **Authy**.

Think of 2FA as a second lock on your digital front door. Even if a hacker steals your password, they still need the temporary code from your second device. This drastically reduces the chance of unauthorized access.

Enable 2FA on your email, banking apps, social media accounts, cloud storage, and anywhere else that offers it. Avoid using SMS-based 2FA if possible, as phone numbers can be hijacked through SIM-swapping attacks. Authenticator apps or physical security keys like **YubiKey** are more secure.

Training Yourself to Think Like a Password Pro

Cybersecurity isn't just about tools — it's about mindset. Begin treating your login credentials like cash. You wouldn't leave hundred-dollar bills lying around your apartment or office, yet many people store passwords in unencrypted text files or notes apps. Train yourself to question every login attempt: Am I on the correct website? Is this a secure connection? Has this password been reused?

Take small steps daily. Audit your current passwords using a password checker. Replace your most vulnerable logins with stronger ones. Set calendar reminders to update key passwords quarterly. Use 2FA wherever possible. And most importantly, stop assuming "it won't happen to me."

Protecting your logins is the most basic yet most critical habit in cybersecurity. With just a few upgrades to your password hygiene, you'll be significantly more secure than the average user — and far less likely to fall victim to the next breach or scam.

Passwords, Passphrases & Protecting Your Logins

Derrick had always thought of himself as a "tech guy." He

managed his own e-commerce website, ran several online accounts for product suppliers, and stored everything from invoices to product photos in cloud folders. He wasn't a cybersecurity expert by any means, but he was careful—or so he thought.

One night, while sipping green tea and updating a product listing, he got locked out of his own site. At first, he assumed it was a glitch. Maybe his session expired. But when he tried to log in again, his password didn't work. He clicked "Forgot Password" and waited for the reset email. Nothing came. He tried again. Still nothing.

He opened his email app. That, too, was locked. Panic crept in slowly. He reached for his phone, only to find a strange message waiting: *"We've taken control of your accounts. If you want access back, send $500 in Bitcoin."* His jaw tightened. In a matter of minutes, someone had stolen his identity online—and Derrick had no idea how.

It didn't take long for the damage to unfold. The hackers had used one of Derrick's old passwords—one he'd created years ago and reused on dozens of sites. When a data breach from a third-party marketing tool exposed user credentials, his login was among them. The attackers simply used that same password on other services, and it worked.

He'd always meant to update his passwords—"later." He knew better than to reuse the same one across multiple platforms, but the convenience outweighed the risk—until now. "Why would anyone target me?" he'd thought. But it turned out, he wasn't targeted. He was just easy.

That one reused password gave hackers access to his PayPal, Gmail, and Shopify accounts. They changed recovery emails, redirected customer orders, and began sending phishing emails to his client list. Derrick spent the rest of the night calling his bank, freezing cards, and trying to get his accounts back before the damage became irreversible.

In the days that followed, Derrick went down a cybersecurity rabbit hole. He learned about **credential stuffing**, where bots test stolen passwords across thousands of sites in seconds. He discovered that most hackers didn't need to "break in"—they just walked through open doors.

He found out how easy it was to download leaked credentials from old breaches, some dating back a decade. Many of those emails and passwords still worked today because users never changed them. Derrick even found his old password posted on a breach database. His stomach turned.

Determined to take back control, he deleted every weak or duplicate password and created long, random passphrases for each account. Instead of using short words or birthdays, he now used phrases like *"Pineapple$Drums*Fly1994!"* or *"CoffeeBooks&JazzForever."* They were long, unusual, and easy to remember—but impossible to guess. He added two-factor authentication to every platform that supported it, vowing to never underestimate digital hygiene again.

Derrick also discovered password managers. At first, he was skeptical—wasn't putting all your passwords in one place dangerous? But the more he researched, the more he realized that **encrypted password managers** were far safer than relying on memory or notebooks. He chose one that offered zero-knowledge encryption and synced securely across his devices.

Now, Derrick only needed to remember **one** master passphrase. The manager generated and stored all the rest. What once felt like a headache became automatic. Every time he visited a site, the login fields filled themselves with powerful, unique credentials. He began to feel—finally—in control.

He went a step further. He checked every account to see if it had 2FA options and used an authenticator app instead of SMS, which he learned could be compromised through

SIM-swapping. With a few hours of effort, he turned his scattered, vulnerable login system into a fortress.

One afternoon, Derrick got a new client—someone who had been referred by a friend in the e-commerce space. During their onboarding call, the client mentioned they'd recently been locked out of their Instagram business account and lost thousands in potential sales.

Derrick listened carefully, recognizing the symptoms. It was the same thing that had happened to him just a few weeks earlier. Instead of simply sympathizing, he walked the client through setting up a password manager, creating strong passphrases, and enabling 2FA. The client was stunned by how simple the fixes were—and how few people actually took the time to do them.

What had started as a personal disaster was now becoming a professional asset. Derrick began offering **digital security checkups** as a service to his other clients. He created templates for strong password creation and gave mini-trainings on account protection. His past mistake had become a powerful part of his brand—and his recovery story.

Looking back, Derrick knew that a single reused password had nearly cost him everything. He lost over $1,200 in canceled orders, had to refund clients, and spent two weeks recovering accounts. But in a strange way, it was also the best wake-up call he could've asked for. Today, Derrick feels different when logging in. No more reused credentials. No more easy targets. His business is secure, his clients are protected, and his habits are sharp. He knows cybersecurity isn't just for corporations or governments—it starts with small, personal decisions.

And for Derrick, it all started with learning that a strong password isn't just a key—it's the lock that keeps everything else safe.

Chapter 3: Recognizing Scams, Phishing, and Social Engineering Attacks

Why Cybercriminals Don't Hack, They Trick

Cybersecurity threats often don't begin with broken firewalls or high-tech malware. They begin with deception. One of the most effective and dangerous tools in a hacker's arsenal is not code, but manipulation. **Social engineering** is the art of tricking someone into giving up sensitive information or granting access to systems — all without the attacker needing to force their way in. These attacks exploit human nature, not machines. They rely on urgency, fear, trust, and curiosity to bypass your digital defenses. In fact, phishing and social engineering account for the **majority of successful breaches**, proving that the human mind — not just the system — must be protected.

Phishing Explained: The Bait and Hook of the Digital World

Phishing is the most common form of social engineering. It typically involves fraudulent emails, texts, or messages that appear to come from a trusted source, such as your bank, a major retailer, or even someone in your contacts list. These messages often urge immediate action: "Click here to verify your account," "Your password was compromised — change it now," or "We detected unusual activity on your card." They might link to a website that looks exactly like your bank's login page — but it's fake. Once you enter your credentials, they're sent directly to the attacker.

These scams are evolving rapidly. Today's phishing messages may include personal information, company logos, even full email threads. The goal is to create a false sense of legitimacy. One click or reply is often all it takes to hand over control of your digital identity. Recognizing the red flags — poor grammar, suspicious links, unexpected attachments, and messages that pressure you to act fast — is your first line of defense.

Variants of Phishing: Spear Phishing, Smishing, and Vishing

Not all phishing attacks are broad or generic. Some are targeted and tailored. This type is called spear phishing, where the attacker researches a specific individual or organization and crafts messages designed just for them. These are harder to detect because they appear relevant and often reference real projects, people, or departments. For example, a message might seem to come from your HR department asking for updated direct deposit info. One wrong move, and your paycheck ends up in a hacker's account.

Other phishing formats include smishing (phishing via SMS text messages) and vishing (voice phishing via phone calls). A smishing attack might pretend to be a delivery notice or a bank fraud alert. A vishing call might pose as tech support or IRS enforcement. These methods are especially dangerous because they catch people off guard – they feel real and urgent, and most victims never stop to verify them.

Understanding that phishing now spans across email, phone, text, and even social media helps you stay alert on all fronts.

Social Engineering Tactics and Why They Work

Social engineering attacks aren't just about fake messages. They're psychological. Attackers exploit emotions like fear, excitement, authority, or helpfulness. Some pretend to be a colleague locked out of their account. Others pretend to be a client in a rush. Some pretend to be you.

The most dangerous aspect of social engineering is how ordinary it feels. You may receive a call from someone claiming to be from IT who asks for your login details to "update the system." Or someone might email you pretending to be your CEO, asking you to purchase gift cards for a "client meeting." These attacks succeed not because people are ignorant, but because the request seems routine.

What makes social engineering dangerous is its flexibility — it doesn't rely on malware or advanced code. It relies on you saying yes, clicking too fast, or assuming legitimacy without checking.

How to Detect and Respond to Suspicious Activity

Defending against phishing and social engineering starts with skepticism. Don't assume every email, message, or call is legitimate — even if it looks familiar. Always double-check the sender's address. Hover over links to preview their destination. If the domain looks suspicious or has slight misspellings (like "paypa1.com" instead of "paypal.com"), don't click. Instead of using links in messages, visit the website directly by typing the URL.

If something feels off, pause. Don't act under pressure. Take a few minutes to verify. Call the sender directly using a known number. Report suspicious messages to your IT department, email provider, or security platform.

Modern email systems often filter spam and phishing attempts, but no filter is perfect. Stay alert, especially when the message involves money, passwords, or urgent requests. If you do fall for an attack, act fast: change your passwords immediately, notify your bank, and report the breach to any affected parties.

Building Your Personal "Human Firewall"

Firewalls and antivirus software protect your devices — but the most powerful defense is between your ears. You are the first and last line of defense. The best way to build a "human firewall" is through awareness and habit. Practice healthy skepticism, limit how much personal info you share online, and treat unexpected messages with caution.

Cybercriminals don't need to break through your systems if they can trick you into unlocking the door. But once you understand how these tactics work — and how to spot them — their power begins to fade. Remember, every scam has one thing in common: it depends on you believing it's real. When you stop falling for the bait, the attackers lose their advantage.

This chapter arms you with the mindset to question, verify, and stay one step ahead. As we move forward, you'll build on this foundation by learning how to secure your devices, browsers, and networks — because protecting your logins and recognizing scams is just the beginning of smart cybersecurity.

The Message That Changed Everything

Janet was a well-organized executive assistant for a fast-growing law firm in Austin. She had a knack for juggling calendars, planning meetings, and keeping her boss on track.

Her inbox was always flooded with emails from vendors, attorneys, and clients — and she prided herself on never missing a beat.

One Friday morning, she received an email marked *Urgent*. It was from David, the managing partner of the firm. Or so it appeared.

The subject line read: *"Need These Gift Cards for Client Meeting Today."* The message inside was short and to the point: *"Janet, I'm in court all morning and can't get away. Can you pick up 5 Apple gift cards ($200 each) and email me the codes before 11 AM? Important client appreciation meeting today — will reimburse you after. Thanks — David."*

Janet didn't think twice. She was used to handling last-minute requests. She grabbed her purse and drove to the nearest store.

By 10:30 AM, she had purchased $1,000 worth of gift cards with her own credit card and emailed the codes back to "David." A few minutes later, she got another email: *"Perfect. One more favor — can you grab five more?"*

Something about that second request made her pause. David was generous, but this seemed excessive. She glanced at the sender's email again and noticed something strange. The email wasn't from his firm address. It was a Gmail address that looked like his name — but with a letter swapped.

Her stomach dropped. She opened a new tab and emailed David's real firm address directly. He replied in less than five minutes: *"I didn't send that. Someone's impersonating me. Do not send anything else."*

Janet's heart sank. She had just been scammed.

She called her credit card company immediately, but the damage was done. The cards had already been used — drained within minutes of sending the codes. The scammers were fast. She felt sick.

Back at her desk, she replayed the moment in her head. The email had felt authentic. It had used David's tone, his sign-off, even the kind of language he'd use in a rush. There were no glaring typos or broken grammar. The pressure, the urgency, the trust — it all seemed real.

Janet wasn't naïve. She knew cybercrime existed. But she never imagined she'd be the weak link. She wasn't hacked. She wasn't careless. She was simply tricked.

That night, she barely slept.

The next week, the firm brought in a cybersecurity consultant to train the staff. Janet sat in the front row, eager to learn how she could have prevented what happened.

The consultant explained that this kind of scam was called **business email compromise**, a form of **social engineering**. It didn't rely on breaking through a firewall or planting malware. It relied on human behavior — assumptions, routine, and misplaced trust.

Janet learned about **phishing**, where fake emails are sent in bulk to lure victims. She learned about **spear phishing**, which is more targeted — like the one she'd received. The attacker had clearly studied the firm, used publicly available information, and mimicked real communication patterns.

She also learned about **spoofing**, where email addresses look almost identical to real ones. The trick, she realized, was in the tiny details — a missing letter, an extra symbol, a slightly different domain.

What struck Janet most was how **normal** the scam felt. It hadn't triggered any alarms in her mind because it didn't feel suspicious. That's exactly what social engineering preyed on: trust, urgency, and lack of verification.

The consultant walked the team through ways to spot phishing attempts. Always check the sender's full email. Don't click on suspicious links. Never send gift cards or payments without verifying by phone or an in-person check. Treat any urgent request involving money or credentials with caution — especially if it bypasses normal procedures.

Janet felt a mix of shame and relief. Shame for falling for it, but relief that she now knew how to spot these tricks in the future. She began sharing her story with others — colleagues, friends, even her family — to prevent them from making the same mistake.

Months later, Janet received another suspicious email. This time, it was from a fake vendor saying her invoice was unpaid and she needed to click a link to confirm details. The tone was off. The link was shortened. And something just didn't sit right.

She didn't click. Instead, she called the real vendor. "No, we didn't send that," they confirmed.

Janet smiled. She had just stopped an attack before it started.

From then on, she thought of cybersecurity not as something technical, but as something **personal**. A mindset. A habit. A skill anyone could build. She no longer felt like a victim — she felt like a digital gatekeeper.

And every time she opened a suspicious email or got an odd request, she remembered: the scam only works if you fall for it. Now, she was ready.

Chapter 4: Securing Your Devices — Phones, Computers, and Tablets

Why Your Devices Are the Most Important Targets

Most people think of cybersecurity as something abstract — firewalls, antivirus, encrypted networks — but in reality, it starts with the devices you use every single day. Your phone, laptop, and tablet are gateways to your email, bank accounts, photos, business files, and identity. If a cybercriminal gains access to your device, they often gain access to everything. That's why device security is the bedrock of all cybersecurity efforts. Whether you're working from home, traveling, or just browsing the internet, securing your personal devices is non-negotiable. Hackers aren't always looking for vulnerabilities in the cloud — they're often just looking for the easiest way into your phone or computer.

Keep Your Software and Operating System Updated

One of the most overlooked yet critical steps in device security is keeping your operating system and apps fully updated. Whether you're using iOS, Android, Windows, or macOS, developers regularly release patches to close security gaps. Hackers love outdated software because it gives them an open door into your system — often using known exploits that have already been fixed in newer versions. When you ignore those update notifications or keep clicking "remind me later," you're leaving your device exposed.

Make it a habit to update all your devices weekly. Turn on automatic updates wherever possible, especially for your operating system, browsers, and core apps like email or cloud storage. Updated software doesn't just improve performance – it fixes vulnerabilities that cybercriminals actively search for.

Strengthen Your Lock Screen and Login Settings

Your first line of defense is your lock screen. It's your digital front door. Weak lock screen protections make it easy for anyone – a thief, coworker, or stranger – to access your data in seconds. Always enable screen lock on all devices, and use the strongest method available. On phones and tablets, avoid simple 4-digit PINs. Use a long passcode, fingerprint, or facial recognition where supported.

For laptops and desktops, use a strong password or passphrase to log in and enable full disk encryption (such as BitLocker on Windows or FileVault on macOS). These settings prevent unauthorized users from accessing your files if the device is lost or stolen. Also, configure your screen to auto-lock after a few minutes of inactivity. You should never leave a device accessible and unattended – even for just a moment –

without some kind of lock in place.

Install Security Software and Enable Firewalls

No device should be operating in today's world without proper antivirus and firewall protection. Even though modern operating systems include some built-in protection, it's not always sufficient. Use a trusted antivirus program to detect and block malware, ransomware, and spyware. Many reputable options also include real-time monitoring, email protection, and safe-browsing alerts.

Equally important is your firewall — a digital gatekeeper that monitors incoming and outgoing traffic. Make sure your firewall is turned on in your system settings. This stops unauthorized data from reaching your device and prevents malicious programs from "phoning home" to a hacker's server.

Mobile devices should also be equipped with anti-malware apps, especially if you install apps outside of official app stores. If you're on Android, be extra cautious about permissions and app origins. Never sideload apps unless you're certain of the source.

Secure Your Wi-Fi and Avoid Public Networks

Your device is only as secure as the network it connects to. Home Wi-Fi networks should be password protected with strong WPA3 or WPA2 encryption. Change the default router password (the one printed on the box) and create a new, secure password. Also, rename your network (SSID) to something generic — avoid using names that reveal your identity or location.

When you're on the go, public Wi-Fi can be a major risk. Coffee shops, airports, and hotels often offer unsecured networks that can be easily exploited by cybercriminals using man-in-the-middle attacks. If you must use public Wi-Fi, never access sensitive accounts like banking or work-related tools without protection. The safest option is to use a Virtual Private Network (VPN), which encrypts your internet traffic and masks your location. VPNs are essential tools for securing your connection, especially on mobile devices and laptops.

Backup Regularly and Prepare for Device Loss or Theft

Even with all security measures in place, no system is invincible. Devices can be lost, stolen, or compromised. That's why you must create regular, automated backups of your data. Use both local backups (to an external hard drive) and cloud backups to ensure redundancy. Services like iCloud, Google Drive, OneDrive, or Dropbox offer encrypted cloud storage that automatically backs up important files, photos, and documents.

Additionally, set up remote tracking and device-wiping features. Both Apple and Android devices allow you to locate a missing phone and wipe its contents remotely. Windows and macOS also have options to erase lost devices or lock them from afar. These tools offer a last line of defense — if your device falls into the wrong hands, at least your data won't.

In summary, securing your devices isn't about becoming paranoid — it's about becoming prepared. A few smart changes to your settings and habits can dramatically reduce your risk. Your phone and computer hold your life's data. Protect them like you would protect your wallet, your home, or your identity — because, in many ways, they are all the same.

The Forgotten Laptop

Luis had just finished a long workday at a crowded airport café. As a freelance graphic designer, he often worked wherever he could find a power outlet and a decent cup of coffee. That day, he had been updating a client's pitch deck while waiting for a delayed flight to Miami.

In a rush to get to the gate, he packed up his headphones, unplugged his phone, and slung his backpack over one shoulder. What he didn't realize — until he was buckled into seat 14A — was that he had left something behind: his laptop.

He shot up in his seat and reached for the overhead compartment, heart pounding. But it was too late. The doors were shut. The plane was backing away. His MacBook — with three client projects, personal photos, saved passwords, and login sessions still open — was sitting on a café table next to a half-empty coffee cup.

For the entire flight, Luis spiraled. He had no lock screen timeout. His laptop opened directly to the desktop. His browser remembered all his logins. His passwords were stored in sticky notes on his desktop. His heart sank deeper as he realized just how vulnerable he had made himself.

As soon as the wheels hit the tarmac, he called the airport lost and found. They hadn't seen it. He called the café. No answer. He opened the "Find My" app, only to realize he had never enabled it on that particular Mac. His last hope was to log in to his cloud backup. But even that had failed him — the last time he'd run a full backup was months ago.

Luis stared at his phone, feeling like someone had broken into his house. Only this time, it was his digital house — and he had left the front door wide open.

By the next day, one of his clients emailed him, asking why someone from a foreign IP address had tried to log into their shared folder. Another emailed saying their account was now locked after too many password attempts. Panic turned to guilt.

Luis called a tech-savvy friend named Brianna, who didn't sugarcoat her response: "You didn't secure your device. You basically handed over the keys to everything you own."

Together, they worked to change every password he could remember. They removed access tokens from cloud storage, enabled two-factor authentication where possible, and notified his clients. But the damage had already begun. He lost a client. His credibility took a hit. And his trust in his own habits was completely shattered.

Determined never to feel that helpless again, Luis started from scratch. He bought a new laptop and configured it like a fortress. He enabled full-disk encryption, created a long passphrase login, and set the screen to lock automatically after five minutes of inactivity. He installed antivirus software and turned on the firewall.

He set up cloud backups that would run daily and tested restoring files to make sure they actually worked. He also subscribed to a password manager and wiped every password sticky note from his life. The days of casual convenience were over. Now, it was about control.

But the biggest shift came from his mindset. He no longer viewed security settings as optional or annoying. He saw them as essential – like putting on a seatbelt or locking his front door.

Luis began sharing his story in online freelancer groups. To his surprise, dozens of others admitted they also didn't use lock screens or backup data. Some had never even heard of full-disk encryption. A few had experienced similar losses but hadn't shared them publicly.

He wrote a blog post titled *"I Lost My Laptop – and Nearly My Business"*, which went viral in digital nomad communities. Readers appreciated his honesty and the checklist he included at the end: how to secure devices, create proper backups, and protect client files.

Luis turned his mistake into a mission. He even began offering a "device security review" as an upsell to clients in tech and design – not because he was a cybersecurity expert, but because he had lived through what happens when you ignore it.

Months later, Luis was sitting in another airport, laptop open, finishing a project with confidence. His laptop was locked, encrypted, and backed up. His browser didn't auto-login. His VPN was on. If something happened now – if he lost the device or someone tried to access it — he knew he had layers of protection in place.

He smiled to himself, not because he was fearless, but because he was prepared.

Luis had learned a hard truth: cybersecurity doesn't start with complicated tools or expensive software. It starts with your everyday habits. Your phone, your laptop — they carry your entire life. Protecting them isn't just smart. It's survival in the digital age.

And now, Luis would never forget that again.

Chapter 5: Safe Internet Browsing and Securing Your Online Activity

The Internet Is Not Automatically Safe

Browsing the internet has become second nature — like breathing in the digital world. But every time you go online, you're entering a space full of both incredible opportunities and hidden dangers. Hackers, advertisers, scammers, and data brokers are all competing to collect your information, monitor your behavior, or trick you into clicking something harmful. The assumption that "as long as I don't visit bad websites, I'm safe" is dangerously outdated. Cyber threats are embedded even in seemingly trusted platforms, ads, downloads, and search results. That's why developing safe browsing habits is critical — not just for tech professionals, but for anyone who uses the internet daily.

Choose Secure and Privacy-Focused Browsers

Your browser is your primary window to the internet, and some are safer than others. While Chrome, Safari, Firefox, and Edge are all popular, they differ in how they handle privacy and security. Firefox and Brave, for example, offer built-in tracking protection and stronger privacy features than Chrome, which is deeply tied to Google's data collection systems. Choosing a browser that prioritizes security gives you an immediate advantage.

No matter which browser you use, always keep it updated. New versions patch known vulnerabilities that cybercriminals often exploit. Avoid using outdated browsers or unsupported versions, and disable or remove unnecessary plugins and extensions. Some extensions — even those from official stores — contain malicious code that tracks your activity or injects harmful scripts into websites you visit.

Recognize Malicious Sites and Dangerous Links

One of the most effective cyberattack methods is tricking users into visiting fake or dangerous websites. These sites may look identical to real ones — like your bank, your email provider, or a popular retailer — but they're designed to steal your credentials or install malware. Always double-check the web address before entering sensitive information. A secure site should begin with "https://" and have a padlock icon in the address bar. Still, those indicators aren't foolproof.

Avoid clicking on suspicious pop-ups, fake "Download" buttons, or banner ads that promise free prizes. Use browser settings or extensions to block pop-ups and prevent redirects to unsafe domains. If you receive a link in an email or message, don't click it blindly. Hover over the link to see the actual destination, and when in doubt, visit the site manually by typing the address yourself.

Public Wi-Fi and the Importance of VPNs

Many people access the internet on public Wi-Fi networks at cafés, airports, or hotels without realizing they're putting their entire session at risk. Public networks are notoriously easy for hackers to exploit, allowing them to intercept traffic, steal login credentials, or install malware through unsecured connections.

The best way to protect yourself is by using a Virtual Private Network (VPN). A VPN encrypts your internet traffic and routes it through a secure server, making it unreadable to anyone on the same network — including potential attackers. Whether you're shopping online, checking your bank account, or just reading the news, a VPN is a critical tool when outside your home network. Choose a reputable paid VPN provider, as many free versions compromise your privacy by logging your activity or showing invasive ads.

Protect Your Online Accounts With Browser Hygiene

Beyond avoiding harmful websites, your browser habits play a huge role in your online safety. Avoid letting your browser remember passwords, especially on shared or public devices.

Use a password manager instead. Clear your cookies and cache regularly to remove stored session data that could be used by attackers or trackers. Log out of sensitive accounts when you're done, and close browser tabs you're no longer using.

Also, pay attention to browser permissions. Some sites ask to access your location, camera, or microphone unnecessarily. Deny those permissions unless absolutely required, and periodically review permission settings in your browser dashboard. Limit what you allow your browser to save, and avoid syncing passwords across devices without encryption.

Build a Smart, Security-First Browsing Habit

Safe browsing isn't about being scared — it's about being smart. Set your default search engine to a privacy-friendly option like DuckDuckGo. Turn off autofill features that store credit card info and personal data. Use browser extensions that block ads, trackers, and malicious scripts, such as uBlock Origin or Privacy Badger.

Every online interaction is an opportunity for attackers to exploit your trust or attention. By slowing down and paying attention to where you go and what you click, you can drastically reduce your exposure to threats. Make security part of your browsing routine: keep your software updated, use a

VPN in public, double-check URLs, and treat your browser like a digital passport — valuable, private, and worth protecting.

The internet isn't going anywhere — and neither are the risks. But with safer habits, smarter tools, and a proactive mindset, you can browse with confidence, privacy, and peace of mind.

The Ad That Wasn't

Naomi was on her lunch break at work, scrolling through her favorite fashion blog when she saw a banner that caught her eye: *"LIMITED TIME OFFER — Get Designer Handbags for $49!"* The ad looked polished, had a well-known brand's logo, and featured a countdown timer urging her to act fast.

Curious and excited, she clicked the link.

It led her to a site that looked nearly identical to the official designer website — same fonts, same color scheme, and even customer reviews. She browsed for a few minutes before finding a bag she loved and entered her credit card information, eager to get the deal before it expired.

Later that night, something felt off. She hadn't received a confirmation email. When she went to revisit the website, it was gone. Her heart sank.

The next morning, her bank called to report unusual activity on her card — someone had tried to make multiple purchases overseas. Naomi immediately canceled the card, but the damage was done. The fraudulent site she'd visited wasn't just a scam — it was a **phishing site** built to collect payment data and vanish without a trace.

Ashamed and frustrated, Naomi started Googling terms she never paid attention to before: phishing, spoofed websites, fake ads. She learned that thousands of fraudulent websites are launched every day, often using realistic-looking branding and fake reviews to trick users. They don't need to hack your system — they just need you to trust them.

The irony hit hard: she had always considered herself careful. But the urgency and visual legitimacy of the ad had overridden her instincts.

Naomi called her brother, Alex, a cybersecurity analyst. He wasn't surprised. "That's called malvertising," he explained. "Bad ads get past filters, especially on third-party websites. One click is all it takes."

He asked her what browser she used. "Chrome," she replied. "But I don't think it's updated." He sighed and began walking her through a basic online safety audit.

Together, they changed her browser settings. They installed a secure extension to block pop-up ads and malicious scripts. They added a privacy-focused search engine. He showed her how to manually type in web addresses instead of clicking ads and how to verify site security using HTTPS and the domain spelling.

"You didn't do anything stupid," he reassured her. "You just didn't know the rules. Most people don't."

Naomi began taking internet security seriously. She started paying attention to small details: the way a website's URL looked, how certain links redirected too quickly, or when a deal seemed too good to be true. She stopped clicking random ads altogether and bookmarked her favorite retailers' official websites.

She also installed a **VPN** for browsing while at cafés and airports, learning that public Wi-Fi could be a playground for cyber snoops. With Alex's help, she created a clean browser profile for work and another for personal browsing. She cleared her cookies weekly, disabled autofill on sensitive fields, and stopped saving her credit card details in the browser.

The more she learned, the more confident she felt — and the more surprised she became at how many risky behaviors had once felt totally normal.

One day, a coworker approached her in the breakroom. "Hey, Naomi – you're good with online stuff, right?" He explained that his Instagram account had been locked after clicking a link promising a free pair of sneakers. Naomi nodded. She'd seen this before. "That's probably phishing," she said. "You should change your password right away and turn on two-factor authentication."

She sat with him and walked him through it. By the end of the conversation, he thanked her. "Honestly, I didn't think this stuff was real. I just thought it happened to older folks or people who aren't tech-savvy."

Naomi smiled. "It happens to everyone. The only difference is whether you learn from it or not."

Weeks later, Naomi was browsing online for a birthday gift. She came across another flashy ad for electronics that seemed... off. The price was too low. The domain name was a weird combination of letters. Her mouse hovered over the link, then stopped. She closed the tab and searched for the item directly on a reputable retailer's site.

It felt like a small victory – not just avoiding a scam, but catching it before it had a chance to begin.

From that day forward, Naomi never browsed the same way

again. She understood that the internet wasn't automatically safe — and that security wasn't just about protecting her device, but protecting her decisions. Every click was a choice. And now, she chose wisely.

Chapter 6: Protecting Your Personal Data and Privacy Online

You're Sharing More Than You Think

Every time you browse the internet, post on social media, shop online, or use an app, you're sharing data — sometimes voluntarily, and often without realizing it. Your name, email address, phone number, location, device type, and browsing habits are constantly being tracked and logged by websites, platforms, advertisers, and sometimes even malicious actors. This collection of information is known as your **digital footprint**, and it follows you across the web. What seems like harmless behavior — liking a post, using a store's mobile app, signing up for a free trial — gradually creates a highly detailed profile about you. Understanding this is the first step to regaining control over your online privacy.

Limit the Data You Give Away

One of the simplest ways to protect your data is to **share less** of it. That means thinking twice before filling out online forms, signing up for newsletters, or allowing apps to access your contacts, camera, or location. Always ask yourself: Do they really need this information? Many websites and services ask for far more than is necessary.

Start by minimizing the personal information you post on social media. Avoid sharing your birthday, full home address, or travel plans in real time. Don't overshare in "fun" quizzes or viral polls — many are disguised phishing tools designed to harvest details for security questions or scam targeting. When creating accounts, use pseudonyms or initials where possible, and use an email alias (or throwaway email) for non-essential sign-ups.

Manage App Permissions and Device Privacy Settings

Your devices are loaded with apps that constantly request access to personal information. On your phone, go to your settings and check which apps have access to your microphone, camera, GPS, contacts, and storage. Disable permissions that aren't absolutely necessary for the app to function. A flashlight app doesn't need your GPS. A calculator doesn't need your contact list.

On both Android and iOS, you can now choose to allow apps to access location **only while in use**, or **never**. Take advantage of this. Also, disable ad tracking wherever possible in your device settings. These settings limit how much advertisers can track you across apps and websites. It won't make you invisible, but it significantly reduces how much data is collected in the background.

Use Privacy-Focused Tools and Browsers

The tools you use matter. Switching to privacy-first browsers like **Brave**, **Firefox**, or **Tor** helps minimize tracking while you browse. These browsers automatically block cookies, scripts, and ads that track your activity. Set your search engine to **DuckDuckGo** or **Startpage**, which don't log your searches or behavior.

Install privacy tools like **uBlock Origin** (for ad blocking), **Privacy Badger** (for invisible tracker detection), and **HTTPS Everywhere** (to force secure connections). These browser extensions work in the background to reduce tracking and block unsafe elements from loading.

Also consider using **email masking tools** like Firefox Relay, Apple's "Hide My Email," or services like SimpleLogin. These tools create alias email addresses that forward to your real inbox, allowing you to sign up for services without exposing your real address.

Understand What Data Brokers Know About You

Data brokers are companies that buy, aggregate, and sell your personal information — including your age, address, income level, buying habits, and even your political views. They collect this from public records, surveys, online purchases, social media behavior, and app usage. This data is then sold to advertisers, insurance companies, employers, and sometimes even scammers.

You can opt out of many of these data brokers, although the process can be tedious. Services like **DeleteMe**, **Incogni**, or **Privacy Bee** help automate the removal of your data from hundreds of broker sites. It's worth doing — especially if you've experienced spam calls, targeted scams, or unwanted tracking.

Remember, the more data that's stored in one place, the more attractive it becomes to hackers. Data breaches happen regularly, and when your information is floating around everywhere, your risk increases. Limiting your exposure reduces your vulnerability.

Build a Long-Term Privacy Habit

Privacy isn't a one-time fix — it's an ongoing mindset. Make it a habit to review your social media privacy settings every few months. Audit your app permissions. Clean out old accounts you no longer use by searching your inbox for "welcome to" or "account created." Use a password manager to generate strong, unique passwords for every account. And turn on **two-factor authentication** for all critical services.

Privacy is a form of digital self-defense. It gives you control over what others know, see, and do with your information. While it's nearly impossible to erase your entire digital footprint, you can significantly reduce its size, visibility, and value to cybercriminals.

In an age where companies profit from your personal data, choosing privacy is an act of empowerment. You don't need to go off the grid — you just need to learn how to move through the digital world with your eyes open, your settings locked, and your personal life protected.

Tracked, Tagged, and Too Exposed

Lena was a teacher, artist, and weekend traveler. She loved sharing her life on social media—especially her spontaneous getaways. Her Instagram was a visual diary of sunsets, iced lattes, museum selfies, and handwritten poems. She had just over 8,000 followers, most of them strangers, but she didn't think much about it. "I'm not famous," she'd laugh. "Who'd want my info?"

One Saturday, she posted a story from a boutique hotel two hours outside the city. She tagged the location, shared her room number by accident in a mirror photo, and posted her usual "Out of Office" auto-response link in her bio.

On Sunday night, she returned home to find her apartment

door slightly open. She froze. Inside, drawers were pulled out. Her laptop was gone. Jewelry, too. The police confirmed: it was a targeted break-in.

The scariest part? There were no signs of forced entry. Whoever had done it knew she wasn't home. And they knew how to find her.

Lena didn't sleep that night. As she scrolled through her own feed, it hit her — she had given them the roadmap. Her posts had shown she was out of town. Her profile listed her city and even her neighborhood. The mirror selfie had reflected her key card. The auto-reply from her email had confirmed she wouldn't be back until Monday.

She thought about every online form she'd filled out, every quiz she took on Facebook, every photo she'd geotagged. It suddenly felt like her entire life was available to anyone who wanted to take a peek — or worse, take advantage.

The next morning, she deleted half her Instagram stories, changed the settings to private, and removed her bio details. But the damage had already been done.

Her friend Malik, a cybersecurity blogger, heard about the break-in and called her immediately. "This wasn't just about physical security," he said. "You've got a digital footprint that's way too big. And I'm guessing you've never cleaned it up."

He walked her through an eye-opening exercise: a reverse lookup using her email address. Dozens of old accounts popped up. A fitness app, a coupon site, an astrology newsletter. She hadn't used most of them in years. Some still had her full name and home address publicly visible.

They searched her name on data broker sites. Within minutes, they found her home address, age, salary estimate, and even a list of her relatives.

Lena felt violated. "How is all of this out there?" she asked.

"It's always been out there," Malik said. "But now, you know where to look — and what to fix."

The next few days were a blur of account deletions, email opt-outs, and privacy setting overhauls. Malik showed her how to use **email masking** so she didn't have to give out her real address when signing up for things. They used **Firefox Relay** and **Apple's Hide My Email** to start separating her real identity from casual accounts.

She cleaned up her phone too — deleting over 40 apps she hadn't used in over a year. She was shocked to learn how many still had background access to her location and microphone. She changed those permissions, turned off ad tracking, and finally turned on two-factor authentication for her bank, email, and photo storage.

Lena also set up a **VPN** for public browsing and installed a browser extension that blocked trackers. For the first time in years, her online experience felt quiet — no personalized ads following her, no retargeting, no endless pop-ups asking for more info.

What started as fear slowly became empowerment. Lena began teaching her students about online privacy. Not from a place of paranoia — but from a place of protection. She explained how to build a healthy digital identity, how to recognize oversharing, and how to turn privacy into a habit.

She also wrote a blog post about her experience, titled *"I Tracked Myself Online — And You Should Too."* It resonated with thousands. People messaged her saying they never realized how much data they had exposed. Some even told her they'd experienced similar close calls.

The break-in had cost her thousands in lost items and peace of mind — but it had also woken her up to something even more valuable: her digital life needed boundaries just as much as her physical one.

Months later, Lena still shared sunsets and poems — but no

locations, no time stamps, and no clues about where she was or what she was doing in real time. Her accounts were private. Her browser was encrypted. And her phone only gave permissions when absolutely necessary.

She didn't disappear from the internet. She just became smarter about how she showed up.

And now, every time she thought about posting something personal, she paused and asked herself one simple question:

"Would I hand this information to a stranger in a parking lot?"

If the answer was no, she didn't post it.

That was Lena's new rule — and it changed everything.

Chapter 7: Securing Your Email, Messaging, and Social Media Accounts

Why Communication Platforms Are Prime Targets

Your email, messaging apps, and social media accounts are more than just tools for connection — they're high-value digital assets. These platforms contain your conversations, private files, contacts, history, and personal data. More importantly, they serve as **gateways** to other services. If someone gains access to your email, for instance, they can often reset your passwords, bypass security questions, and hijack your identity across multiple platforms. That's why these accounts are frequently targeted by hackers. Securing them is not just about protecting messages — it's about protecting your entire digital life.

Email: The Digital Master Key

Start with your email account, especially if you use it to register for banking, shopping, or cloud services. Use a **strong, unique passphrase** for email logins and never reuse that password anywhere else. Enable **two-factor authentication (2FA)** immediately — preferably with an authenticator app like Google Authenticator or Authy, rather than SMS, which can be hijacked via SIM swapping.

Regularly check your email's **security settings and login history** to detect unauthorized access. Set up **email forwarding alerts** – attackers sometimes secretly forward copies of your incoming mail to themselves. Also, avoid linking your recovery options (phone or backup email) to insecure or outdated services. Your recovery method should be just as secure as your primary email itself.

Secure Your Messaging Apps: WhatsApp, Signal, iMessage, Telegram

Modern messaging apps offer end-to-end encryption, but users often forget that **account access** is still vulnerable. WhatsApp and Signal, for instance, are tied to your phone number. If someone clones your SIM card or accesses your backup, they can read your messages or impersonate you.

Enable all available **security settings** within your messaging apps. On WhatsApp, enable **two-step verification**, which adds a PIN required when registering your number on a new device. On Signal and Telegram, set up **registration locks** and screen lock features. On iMessage, make sure iCloud has **two-factor authentication** enabled, and disable auto-login across Apple devices you don't use.

For sensitive conversations, consider using apps like **Signal** or **Session**, which don't store metadata and don't require your phone number.

Social Media Accounts: Limit, Lock, and Monitor

Social media accounts are prime targets for impersonation, harassment, data scraping, and brand hijacking. Start by reviewing all your **privacy settings**. Make your account private or restrict who can view posts, send messages, tag you, or see your friend list. Avoid using your full birthdate, hometown, or other personally identifiable info in your bio.

Enable 2FA wherever possible and set alerts for **suspicious login activity**. Facebook, Instagram, Twitter (X), LinkedIn, and TikTok all have security dashboards that show where your account is logged in and let you log out remotely.

Be cautious of third-party apps that connect to your social media accounts — these often request excessive permissions and can become security liabilities. Revoke access to any apps you no longer use. Avoid clicking on strange links sent via direct messages or comment spam, especially if it promises giveaways, free products, or profile "verifications."

Backup and Recovery Strategies

Even with strong security, no account is invincible. That's why having recovery strategies in place is critical. For email and social platforms, update your recovery email and phone numbers regularly. Store backup codes (given during 2FA setup) in a secure password manager or offline location.

For messaging apps, regularly export important chat backups — but encrypt them if you're storing them in the cloud. Make sure cloud backups are not set to auto-restore to new devices without an authentication step.

On social media platforms, consider downloading a copy of your account data periodically. If you ever lose access or get locked out, this gives you a historical record you can use during recovery. Some platforms (like Instagram and Facebook) now allow you to designate **trusted contacts** who can help with account recovery.

Build Smart Communication Habits

Security tools matter, but habits are just as important. Don't click on links or attachments in unsolicited messages — even if they come from a known contact (their account may have been hacked). Avoid using messaging apps as file storage. Don't send sensitive documents or passwords through unsecured platforms. Never publicly share personal details on social media posts, such as vacation plans, full names of family members, or your workplace's internal processes.

Keep your apps updated. Most security patches are issued

through app updates, and outdated versions can have unpatched vulnerabilities. Use password managers to create strong, unique passwords for each platform — and never share them via chat.

Ultimately, your communication platforms represent your digital voice and identity. If someone else gains access, they can manipulate how you appear, what you say, and who you interact with. Securing these platforms isn't just about privacy — it's about **maintaining trust** in every message, every post, and every conversation.

The Message That Wasn't Me

Travis was a high school coach, part-time podcaster, and the unofficial social media manager for his school's athletic department. He was always online — responding to emails, texting athletes' parents, and posting game-day highlights on Instagram.

One Saturday morning, while checking his inbox, he noticed something strange: dozens of bounce-back emails from addresses he didn't recognize. Some were international. Others looked like spam filters had caught them. Confused, he refreshed his inbox again. That's when his phone buzzed. A colleague messaged: *"Hey, did you mean to send me that weird link on Facebook Messenger?"*

He hadn't.

He opened Messenger and saw messages he didn't write — sent not just to his contacts, but to people he barely knew. The messages were short and suspicious: *"Look at this video of you"* followed by a shady-looking link.

His stomach turned. His accounts had been compromised — and he had no idea how far it had gone.

Travis spent the next three hours frantically changing passwords. But it was too late. His Facebook account had already been flagged for spam. His Instagram posts had vanished. And worst of all, his main email had been used to try and reset his bank login.

"I thought I was being safe," he said out loud, staring at the screen. But he'd never enabled two-factor authentication. His email password — which he used on several platforms — had been exposed in an old data breach from a nutrition app he barely remembered signing up for.

And once the attackers had his email, they used it to access his social media, reset his logins, and start sending messages that looked like they were coming from him.

His reputation was now on the line. He called his friend Daryl, a cybersecurity consultant. Daryl didn't judge. "It happens more often than you'd think," he said. "You didn't just get hacked. You got impersonated. That's worse."

They got to work.

First, Daryl helped him secure his **email account** with a new passphrase and enabled **two-factor authentication** using an authenticator app — not SMS. They checked for **unauthorized logins** and turned off all **auto-forwarding rules** the hacker had set up to siphon off new messages.

Next, they tackled his **Facebook and Instagram** accounts. Daryl walked him through submitting an identity appeal and verified backup email. Thankfully, Travis had enough content and identification to reclaim both accounts.

Then they reviewed all connected apps and revoked access to anything he didn't recognize — including a random quiz site from three years ago that still had permission to post on his behalf.

Daryl then turned their attention to **messaging apps**. WhatsApp, Signal, Telegram — all were tied to Travis's phone number. They updated security settings, enabled **registration locks**, and backed up conversations manually. Travis was shocked to learn how easy it was for someone to hijack his messaging app with just a code and access to his email.

They also downloaded and set up a **password manager**. Travis was finally able to generate strong, unique passwords for every account. No more reusing the same combination from high school.

The final step was awareness. They reviewed **phishing messages**, fake login pages, and suspicious links. Travis realized how easily one click had triggered this entire mess.

He had clicked a fake "Facebook login" email after a late night of editing highlight clips. He thought it was real. The hackers thought he was easy.

Weeks passed. Travis rebuilt his online presence. He posted a short message to his audience explaining what had happened — not to make excuses, but to **warn others**. Dozens of followers thanked him. A few admitted they'd clicked the same message and changed their own passwords just in time.

He also held a short workshop for his students and fellow coaches, walking them through account security settings. Most had never even heard of 2FA. Many were still using weak passwords — or sharing Netflix logins with their email accounts.

"You're not just protecting your accounts," he told them. "You're protecting your name. Your identity. And your trust."

Travis no longer felt embarrassed. He felt equipped. And he wanted others to feel that way too.

Now, every time Travis logs into his email, opens Instagram, or sends a message, he knows his digital door is locked tight.

He checks his login activity monthly. He clears access for apps he doesn't use. He stopped sharing private messages across multiple platforms. And whenever someone sends him a suspicious link — even if it looks like it's from a friend — he pauses.

Because he remembers what it felt like to have his digital voice stolen.

And because the next time someone sends a message pretending to be him, they'll hit a wall — not an open window.

Chapter 8: Protecting Your Children and Family Online

Digital threats don't just target adults — they affect the entire household. Children today are born into a connected world, where screens, apps, and games are as normal as crayons and bicycles. But with that connectivity comes exposure: to predators, scammers, inappropriate content, addictive algorithms, and privacy-invading apps. As a parent or guardian, it's your responsibility to create a **safe and secure digital environment** — one that empowers your family to use technology with confidence and caution. Cybersecurity is no longer optional in parenting. It's a vital skill set for raising safe and digitally responsible children.

Secure Your Home Network and Devices

Start with the basics: protect your home Wi-Fi network. Change the default router password and set a strong, custom passphrase. Use **WPA3 or WPA2 encryption**, and consider hiding the network SSID if you live in a high-density area. You can also set up a separate **guest network** for visitors so they don't access your family's main devices or shared files.

Set **parental controls** on all family devices. Most smartphones, tablets, and computers have built-in tools that let you restrict content, limit screen time, block downloads, and monitor app usage. Enable safe search settings on browsers and YouTube. Install **security software** on every family device — including tablets and smartphones — to protect against phishing, malware, and inappropriate content.

Teach Kids the Fundamentals of Online Safety

Even with all the filters and controls in place, the most powerful defense is education. Talk to your children about the importance of **not sharing personal information** online — no full names, addresses, birthdays, or school names. Emphasize the difference between public and private sharing, and teach them to **ask before posting** photos or videos of others.

Make sure they understand that **strangers online are still strangers**, even if they seem friendly. Role-play scenarios to help them recognize manipulation or inappropriate questions. Teach them how to identify scams and to never click suspicious links — even if they come from someone they know. Create a family rule: if something online makes them feel uncomfortable or unsafe, they should tell a trusted adult immediately.

Manage Apps, Games, and Social Media Access

Apps and games often seem harmless, but many are loaded with in-app purchases, location tracking, and data collection. Always review an app's permissions before allowing your child to install it. Turn off access to the microphone, camera, and location unless absolutely necessary. Use the device's **content rating filters** to ensure your child only sees age-appropriate content.

Delay social media access as long as possible. Most platforms require users to be at least 13 years old, but even then, it's up to parents to determine when their child is ready. If you allow access, help them set up the account. Make profiles private, disable location tags, and review friend requests together. Encourage them to take regular breaks from social media to avoid mental fatigue, bullying, or addictive behavior patterns.

Monitor, Guide, and Set Boundaries

Monitoring your child's online behavior is not about invading their privacy — it's about protecting their safety. Use parental control dashboards to set limits and track online activity, but pair that with regular conversations. Create screen-free zones (such as bedrooms or dinner tables) and set daily screen time limits. Encourage other activities like reading, outdoor play, and face-to-face social time.

Model the behavior you want to see. If you're constantly on your phone or oversharing on social media, kids will mimic that. Show them what healthy digital habits look like. Review digital contracts or family tech agreements that outline clear expectations — like no device use after 9 PM, weekly password checks, and no new app downloads without permission.

Build a Culture of Digital Trust and Responsibility

The goal isn't to scare your children away from the internet — it's to teach them how to navigate it wisely. Create a home culture where **tech use is open, not secretive**. Let your children know that they can talk to you about anything they experience online — without fear of punishment or shame. Praise responsible behavior. Celebrate smart decisions.

Also, extend cybersecurity habits to extended family. Educate grandparents and relatives on not sharing photos of your children publicly without consent. Limit how much personal data the entire household shares through smart speakers, online games, or social platforms.

Cybersecurity is a family value — something that should be passed on just like manners, boundaries, and self-respect. When children grow up knowing how to protect their identity, communicate wisely, and recognize digital dangers, they're not just safer online — they're better prepared for life.

The Secret App

When Karen found a new app on her 11-year-old daughter Mia's tablet called "VaultPic," she thought it was just another photo editor. But something about it felt off. The icon was disguised as a calculator. Curious, she tapped it and was met with a numeric login screen.

After some Googling, Karen learned it wasn't a photo app at all — it was a **hidden storage app** designed to keep videos, photos, and even browser history concealed from parents.

Her heart sank.

She and Mia had always had a trusting relationship. Or so she thought. But this app, and what it represented, suggested her daughter had been exposed to something she wasn't ready to talk about — or didn't feel safe sharing.

Karen knew she had to address it. Not with anger — but with calm, care, and clarity.

That night, Karen sat down with Mia in the living room.

"I noticed a new app on your tablet," she said gently. "I looked it up. Can we talk about it?"

Mia's face flushed. She avoided eye contact. "It's just for pictures," she mumbled.

Karen took a deep breath. "I'm not mad. I just want to understand. What made you want to hide your pictures?"

After a few minutes of silence, Mia finally opened up. A group of girls from school had been sharing makeup tutorials and "body check" videos — clips where they subtly showed off how thin they were. They called it fun. They dared each other to post clips to a private social feed and rate them. The vault app was their way of keeping it hidden from their parents.

Karen felt sick. Not because Mia had broken rules — but because this world, full of quiet pressure and unfiltered access, had crept into her daughter's life so quickly.

The next morning, Karen made a decision: no more assuming her home's digital life was "safe enough." She took action.

First, she updated the **home Wi-Fi password** and set up a **guest network** for visitors. She installed **screen time settings** on Mia's tablet and phone, and turned on **parental filters** across apps, the app store, YouTube, and Safari.

Then, she went through each app on Mia's devices — deleting anything questionable, blocking in-app purchases, and disabling location sharing. Together, they installed a **safe browser** designed for kids.

But Karen didn't stop there. She started an ongoing family

conversation about online privacy, identity, peer pressure, and how easy it is to fall into harmful content disguised as "harmless trends."

Mia didn't resist. In fact, she seemed relieved.

Karen also talked with other parents at school. To her surprise, many had no idea about the vault apps, the anonymous Q&A platforms, or the messaging features buried in seemingly innocent games. Some hadn't checked their kids' phones in months.

She organized a small "digital safety roundtable" for interested parents. Together, they created a simple checklist: secure the home network, update parental controls, disable auto-location, monitor apps, and — most importantly — **talk with your kids regularly** about what they see and do online.

It wasn't about controlling their every move. It was about creating a culture of awareness and accountability.

Karen even gave Mia a role in that. "You're growing up online," she told her. "Let's figure out how to do it together."

Weeks later, Mia came to Karen holding her phone.

"Someone messaged me asking weird questions on that drawing app," she said. "He said he was 14 but... it didn't feel right."

Karen nodded, proud. "You did the right thing by showing me."

They reported the user and deleted the app.

That moment confirmed something Karen had hoped for all along — that the boundaries she'd set weren't walls, but bridges. Mia didn't see her mom as the tech police. She saw her as an ally.

And that, Karen realized, was the whole point.

Their home felt different now. Not restrictive — but smarter.

There were rules: no devices after 8 PM. Screens stayed out of bedrooms. New apps required a conversation and joint review. And every Sunday, they had a "tech talk" over pancakes — where Mia could ask questions, share stories, or bring up anything weird she'd come across online.

Karen didn't know everything about cybersecurity. But she didn't need to. What mattered was showing up, staying involved, and keeping the conversation open.

In the end, the vault app wasn't just a wake-up call. It was the beginning of a better, stronger connection — one where Mia felt safe enough to ask, and Karen felt equipped enough to answer.

That's what digital parenting looked like in the real world.

Chapter 9: Recognizing and Responding to Identity Theft

Understanding What Identity Theft Really Is

Identity theft occurs when someone steals your personal information — such as your Social Security number, credit card number, driver's license, or login credentials — and uses it without your consent, often to commit fraud. This could include opening bank accounts in your name, applying for loans, filing false tax returns, accessing your insurance benefits, or even impersonating you online. The consequences can range from financial loss and damaged credit to legal trouble and emotional stress. In a world where data breaches are increasingly common, learning how to recognize and respond to identity theft is critical for your long-term security and peace of mind.

Early Warning Signs of Identity Theft

Identity theft doesn't always announce itself with dramatic fraud. Often, the clues are subtle. You might notice unauthorized transactions on your credit card, receive strange mail about unfamiliar accounts, or see new inquiries on your credit report. Other red flags include being denied credit when you previously had good standing, receiving calls from debt collectors about unfamiliar bills, or learning that your tax return has already been filed by someone else.

Even small changes — like missing expected bills or suddenly not receiving verification codes — could signal that your address or email has been changed without your permission. Pay attention to all account activity. Identity theft is often detected by those who are vigilant, not by those waiting for disaster.

Immediate Steps to Take If You Suspect Identity Theft

If you suspect you've been targeted, act fast. First, **place a fraud alert** on your credit reports with one of the three major credit bureaus (Equifax, Experian, or TransUnion) — they're required to notify the others. A fraud alert makes it harder for new accounts to be opened in your name without extra verification. Next, **review your credit reports** for unfamiliar accounts or activity.

Report the identity theft to the **Federal Trade Commission (FTC)** at identitytheft.gov. The FTC will generate a personalized recovery plan and a report that you can use to file police reports or dispute accounts. Also, contact any companies where fraud occurred — such as your bank, lender, or utility provider — and ask to freeze or close the compromised accounts. Keep records of every call, report, and case number.

Locking Down Your Information

Once you've contained the immediate threat, it's time to prevent further damage. Change passwords for all affected accounts and any others that use the same or similar login credentials. Use a **password manager** to generate strong, unique passwords. Enable **two-factor authentication (2FA)** on every financial, email, and social platform.

Consider placing a **credit freeze** on your accounts. Unlike a fraud alert, a credit freeze stops any new creditors from accessing your credit report until you manually lift the freeze — a stronger option if you're not planning to open new accounts soon. You can still access your existing credit cards and use your accounts normally, but new applications won't go through without your permission.

Monitor Your Identity Going Forward

Recovery is only half the battle. The real power comes in monitoring and early detection. Sign up for **credit monitoring services** (some are free with major banks or credit card companies). These tools alert you to changes in your credit profile, including new accounts, missed payments, or suspicious inquiries.

Consider using **identity theft protection services** like LifeLock, Aura, or IdentityForce. These services provide dark web scans, data breach alerts, and even insurance coverage for stolen funds or legal fees.

Check your bank statements weekly. Review your credit reports at least once a year (you can get free copies from annualcreditreport.com). Also, keep your Social Security card, birth certificate, and other sensitive documents in a secure, locked location — not your wallet or email inbox.

How to Protect Yourself from Future Attacks

Most identity theft happens because of weak digital habits — using the same password on multiple accounts, clicking phishing emails, sharing sensitive data on public Wi-Fi, or ignoring software updates. Begin implementing strong cybersecurity habits now: use **VPNs on public networks**, avoid sharing personal info on social media, and scrutinize every suspicious message or call.

Be especially cautious with **paper mail**. Shred old documents, especially those containing financial or medical information. Don't leave outgoing mail in your mailbox overnight — it's a prime target for thieves looking for account numbers and personal data.

Teach your family members — especially elderly parents and teenagers — about identity theft. Many cases arise because one family member unknowingly exposes the household's information.

Identity theft can feel like someone has stolen your name, your credit, and your control. But by responding quickly, locking down your data, and forming smarter habits, you can reclaim that control — and make it much harder for anyone to take it from you again.

Not My Name, Not My Debt

Anthony had just received a job offer. It was his dream role at a fast-growing fintech startup — better pay, remote flexibility, and a generous signing bonus. Everything was falling into place.

But during the background check, HR called with a concerning issue. "Your credit report shows several defaulted accounts — including an auto loan and a department store card. Were you aware of these?"

Anthony's heart stopped.

"No," he said quietly. "That's not mine."

He logged in to his credit report that evening – something he hadn't done in months. There they were: multiple accounts opened under his name. The balances were past due. One account showed an address in a state he'd never lived in.

He wasn't a victim of fraud. He was a victim of identity theft. And he had no idea how far it had gone.

Anthony spent the next two hours on the phone with Equifax, Experian, and TransUnion. He placed a **fraud alert** on his credit profile, flagged the accounts in question, and requested his full credit reports.

Then he visited identitytheft.gov and filed an official report. The FTC website walked him through a personalized recovery plan – including how to file a police report, dispute fraudulent charges, and notify affected companies.

By the end of the night, he had ten case numbers, six PDFs, and a bitter taste in his mouth.

How had this happened?

The more he thought about it, the clearer it became. Months earlier, he had clicked a fake PayPal login page. It looked real. He had entered his credentials. Later, he got a phishing email pretending to be from his bank. He ignored the slight grammar errors and clicked a "confirm identity" link. He remembered thinking something felt off — but he never followed up.

Now, he was paying the price.

The next few weeks were exhausting. Anthony called credit card companies to close fraudulent accounts. Some were helpful. Others were skeptical. He filed a report with local police, not because they would find the culprit — but to generate an official document he could send to creditors.

He also contacted the IRS after hearing stories about **tax fraud** involving stolen identities. Thankfully, no false returns had been filed — but they placed a flag on his file, just in case.

Anthony froze his credit at all three bureaus. No one — including him — could open new lines of credit without lifting the freeze. It gave him a sense of control in a situation that had stripped him of it.

His job offer was put on hold while the background check was sorted. The company wasn't pulling the offer, but they needed "a few more weeks to verify everything."

He'd waited years for this job. Now, because of someone else's actions, that future was in jeopardy.

Determined to prevent this from ever happening again, Anthony changed every password he had. He installed a **password manager**, created long, unique passphrases, and enabled **two-factor authentication** on all critical accounts.

He signed up for an **identity theft monitoring service** that scanned the dark web for any mention of his Social Security number, driver's license, or financial data. The results were shocking. His information had been exposed in three different data breaches — including one from a major hotel chain.

He called his parents and walked them through a cybersecurity checklist. They'd never checked their credit reports. His mom still used her birthdate as her bank password.

"This isn't just about me," he told them. "Anyone can be targeted."

Months later, Anthony received the final confirmation letters. The fraudulent accounts were removed. His credit score began to recover. The fintech company moved forward with onboarding.

But something inside him had changed.

He no longer trusted that "private" meant protected. He started reviewing bank transactions weekly. He taught a lunch-and-learn on identity theft for his new coworkers. He even helped a friend catch a phishing attempt before it turned into a financial mess.

Most importantly, he no longer ignored red flags. If a message looked off, he verified it. If an app requested too many permissions, he didn't install it. If a site didn't use HTTPS, he closed the tab.

Anthony had gone from victim to watchdog.

One morning, he received an alert: someone had attempted to open a retail account using his name. The credit freeze blocked it instantly. No damage done.

He smiled, satisfied. This time, he was ready.

Anthony's story was a hard lesson — one that cost him sleep, time, and opportunity. But it also gave him something more powerful: **awareness**.

He now understood that identity isn't just about your name. It's about how your data is managed, shared, and protected. And in a digital world, **that identity is yours to defend** — every day.

Chapter 10: Building a Lifelong Cybersecurity Mindset

Cybersecurity Is a Lifestyle, Not a Checklist

Too many people view cybersecurity as a one-time setup — install an antivirus, change a few passwords, enable two-factor authentication, and you're done. But in reality, cybersecurity is not just a task. It's a **mindset** — a way of thinking that integrates digital safety into your everyday life. Threats evolve constantly, and so must your awareness. Whether you're at home, traveling, shopping online, or working remotely, your ability to think critically and act cautiously online determines your level of protection. A lifelong cybersecurity mindset turns reaction into prevention.

Stay Informed Without Becoming Overwhelmed

One of the biggest challenges of cybersecurity is staying up to date. New scams, phishing techniques, and malware campaigns emerge daily. But staying informed doesn't mean becoming paranoid or constantly anxious. It means building a healthy awareness and making **education a habit**. Subscribe to a trusted cybersecurity newsletter, listen to monthly podcasts, or follow alerts from organizations like the **FTC**, **CISA**, or **Krebs on Security**.

Make it part of your weekly routine to skim articles or news summaries. The more familiar you become with current threats and tactics, the better you'll spot them in real life. Think of it like brushing your teeth — small, consistent action prevents long-term damage.

Teach Others and Strengthen the "Human Firewall"

One of the most powerful ways to build your cybersecurity mindset is to **share it**. Help your family, coworkers, and friends understand common digital threats. Most breaches don't happen because of advanced technology — they happen because someone clicked the wrong link or used a weak password. These are human errors, and they're preventable.

The more people in your circle who know how to recognize a phishing email, update their software, or use a password manager, the safer **everyone** becomes. You don't need to be a tech expert to make an impact. Just sharing what you've learned can go a long way in creating a "human firewall" — the collective behavior of alert, informed individuals who act as the first line of defense.

Build Cybersecurity Into Daily Habits

Start embedding security into your daily routines. Every time you create a new login, use your password manager. When you're on public Wi-Fi, open your VPN. When you get an unexpected message with a link, verify the source first. When you get a software update notification, install it.

Practice the "pause and verify" technique. Before entering information, ask: Is this a secure site? Is this message really from my bank? Does this download seem suspicious? These micro-decisions take seconds, but they dramatically reduce your risk of compromise.

Also, make time every quarter for a digital cleanup: review your app permissions, delete unused accounts, clear browser history, and rotate key passwords. Think of it like spring cleaning for your digital life.

Balance Convenience and Security

We all crave convenience. Autofill logins, smart home devices, and one-click purchases make life easier. But with every convenience comes a potential cost. A strong cybersecurity mindset means **recognizing the tradeoff** and making intentional choices. That might mean taking an extra 30 seconds to log in with two-factor authentication. It might mean disabling location tracking or choosing not to save your credit card in a browser.

You don't need to eliminate all convenience — but you should know **where the line is**. Always ask: Is the convenience worth the exposure? Can I add a layer of protection without sacrificing usability? Smart decisions create the balance between comfort and control.

Evolve With the Threat Landscape

Cybersecurity is never finished. As technology advances — from smart homes and wearable tech to AI-powered fraud — your mindset must adapt. What works today may be outdated tomorrow. Commit to **continuous improvement**. Learn the basics now, but stay flexible and curious about what's coming next.

Also, prepare for the unexpected. Know what to do if your data is stolen, your accounts are breached, or your identity is compromised. Have a written backup plan, secure offline copies of recovery codes, and a trusted contact you can consult in emergencies.

The most important part of a cybersecurity mindset is the belief that you are **capable**. You don't need to be a coder, hacker, or tech wizard to protect yourself. You just need to care enough to take action.

Because the safest people online aren't the ones who know the most — they're the ones who never stop learning.

The Shift

Priya didn't think much about cybersecurity – until the day she almost lost her freelance business.

It started with a small mistake. She was working from her favorite café, sipping chai and updating a proposal when a Wi-Fi login page popped up. It looked like the café's usual portal, so she entered her email and clicked "Connect."

Nothing seemed wrong.

But later that night, she noticed her Gmail account had logged in from an unfamiliar location. Then her Dropbox password stopped working. Then her website's backend locked her out.

Within hours, someone had gained access to her email, cloud storage, and portfolio site – the core of her business. The intruder didn't wipe anything, but they left behind enough chaos to cause a week's worth of stress and client panic.

Priya hadn't been hacked by brute force. She'd been careless – and that was all it took.

She spent the next few days cleaning up the mess. Changing passwords. Restoring backups. Answering awkward emails from clients who had received suspicious messages. It was exhausting.

She kept asking herself: *Why did I connect to that network without thinking? Why did I reuse the same password on so many platforms?*

That week was her wake-up call.

She started watching YouTube tutorials and reading blog posts about online security. She discovered the concept of the "human firewall." It resonated with her deeply — that most cyberattacks didn't happen because of high-tech hackers, but because someone like her didn't pause to verify a link or thought "it'll never happen to me."

She decided she'd never let herself be that vulnerable again.

At first, she was overwhelmed. There was so much to learn. VPNs, password managers, phishing patterns, dark web monitoring, firewalls... it felt like a foreign language.

But Priya didn't give up. She took it one change at a time.

She started using a **password manager**, which felt like magic. She replaced all her reused passwords with complex, unique ones and enabled **two-factor authentication** everywhere. She updated her browser settings to block trackers and started using **Brave** for privacy.

She turned on automatic updates for her devices. She stopped connecting to public Wi-Fi without using a **VPN**. She began backing up important files in both the cloud and an encrypted external drive.

Each step gave her a little more confidence — not just in her digital life, but in herself.

Her behavior started to change too. When she got an unexpected text message with a link, she didn't click it. When a client sent a strange invoice, she called to confirm. She paused before giving apps access to her camera or microphone. She reviewed privacy settings on social media and removed dozens of old posts that revealed too much.

Cybersecurity was no longer a list of chores. It was a mindset — and it was becoming part of who she was.

One day, she wrote a blog post called *"Cybersecurity for Creatives: Why Your Portfolio Isn't Safe by Default."* It went viral in her niche. Graphic designers, writers, and photographers messaged her, thanking her for breaking it down in a way they could understand.

She started doing Zoom workshops for freelance communities. "You don't need to be an expert," she told them. "You just need to care enough to learn."

What surprised Priya most wasn't how much she learned – it was how **simple the changes were**, once she understood the why behind them. The hardest part had been getting started.

Now, she did a "digital deep clean" every quarter. She reviewed permissions. Deleted unused accounts. Rotated passwords. Scanned for her email on data breach sites. It became as routine as filing taxes or updating her resume.

Cybersecurity became her quiet superpower.

And when her sister called one evening, panicked after receiving a scam phone call asking for her Social Security number, Priya calmly walked her through what to do. "They were trying to social engineer you," she explained. "You did the right thing by hanging up."

Her sister was shocked. "When did you get so good at this?"

Priya smiled. "After I almost lost everything."

Years later, Priya would reflect on that one moment in the café as the pivot point – the day she began to think differently.

She no longer lived in fear of data breaches or online scams. She was aware, prepared, and proactive. Cybersecurity wasn't something she did once. It was something she lived every day.

And it didn't make her feel paranoid.

It made her feel **in control**.

Because in the digital age, safety isn't just about antivirus software or encrypted emails. It's about developing the **habit of awareness** – the ability to pause, question, verify, and adapt.

That's the mindset Priya chose.

And that mindset changed everything.

Epilogue: A Safer You Starts Now

If you've made it to this point, congratulations. You've taken the first — and most important — step toward protecting your digital life: **awareness**. The internet has changed how we live, work, and connect. But with that power comes responsibility. No longer can we afford to treat cybersecurity as someone else's job, or assume that security settings we "set and forget" years ago are still enough. The truth is, cyber threats don't sleep. But neither does your ability to outsmart them.

You don't need to become a tech genius or cybersecurity analyst to stay safe online. You simply need to remain alert, adopt smart habits, and stay curious. Every story in this book showed real-world examples of everyday people — business owners, parents, freelancers, students — who were targeted not because they were famous, but because they were connected. Just like you.

The digital world rewards speed, convenience, and constant sharing. But those same qualities can also expose us. One click, one reused password, one unverified link — that's often all it takes to become a victim. That's why cybersecurity isn't a software problem. It's a **human decision problem**. And the good news is, humans can learn. And you already have.

This book didn't just give you tips. It gave you a **framework**: secure your devices, protect your accounts, recognize scams, back up your data, think critically, and share what you know with those you care about. If you do those things consistently — not perfectly — you'll already be safer than 90% of the population.

You've now built a foundation. The challenge ahead is **keeping it strong**.

Cybersecurity isn't a destination. It's a lifestyle. As new threats evolve — from AI-generated phishing to biometric spoofing to deepfake impersonation — your job is to adapt, not panic. Stay calm, stay informed, and when you don't understand something, take five minutes to research it. Most of the time, that pause is all you need to spot the scam or secure the setting.

Don't be discouraged if you forget a step or let your guard down. What matters is your commitment to **course-correct**. You'll get smarter with every article, every update, every awareness moment. Think of your digital hygiene the same way you think of locking your front door, washing your hands, or buckling your seatbelt. It's not dramatic. It's just smart.

If you're a parent, teach your kids early. If you're a manager, train your team. If you're part of a community, share the simple truths you've learned here. Most people don't fall victim to cybercrime because they're dumb. They fall victim because no one ever taught them what to look for.

But now that you know, you're in a position to **lead by example**.

You can be the reason your household is safer. You can be the voice in the meeting that reminds everyone to verify links before clicking. You can be the friend who tells others how to freeze their credit, report phishing, or recover a stolen identity. One conversation can change someone's life — or save their digital one.

And when you do get frustrated — when passwords feel overwhelming, when privacy feels impossible — remember: **you're not powerless**. You're better prepared than most. And that preparation gives you leverage.

Cybersecurity doesn't mean you'll never be targeted. It means you'll know what to do when you are.

So take a moment to appreciate how far you've come. From learning how scammers operate to hardening your passwords and protecting your kids online, you've gained skills that most people never will. You didn't just listen. You transformed how you think.

That's the real win.

As you close this book, remember this final truth: Cybersecurity isn't just about defense. It's about **empowerment**. You own your data. You control your online identity. You set the tone for your digital boundaries.

And now, you're ready to defend them — not with fear, but with confidence.

So go forward not just as a user of technology... but as its master.

Because in a world where data is power, you just became stronger than ever.

www.ingramcontent.com/pod-product-compliance
Lightning Source LLC
LaVergne TN
LVHW022010200926
848481LV00007B/2322
* 9 7 9 8 3 4 9 6 4 4 6 4 1 *